What can I ...?
See

Sue Barraclough

Heinemann
LIBRARY

www.heinemann.co.uk/library
Visit our website to find out more information about **Heinemann Library** books.

To order:
☎ Phone 44 (0) 1865 888066
▤ Send a fax to 44 (0) 1865 314091
💻 Visit the Heinemann Bookshop at www.heinemann.co.uk/library to browse our catalogue and order online.

First published in Great Britain by Heinemann Library, Halley Court, Jordan Hill, Oxford OX2 8EJ, part of Harcourt Education.
Heinemann is a registered trademark of Harcourt Education Ltd.

Editorial: Sarah Shannon and Louise Galpine
Design: Jo Hinton-Malivoire and Tokay,
    Bicester, UK (www.tokay.co.uk)
Picture Research: Melissa Allison
Production: Camilla Smith

Originated by Chroma Graphics (Overseas) Pte.Ltd
Printed and bound in China by South China Printing Company

ISBN 0 431 02204 6 (hardback)
09 08 07 06 05
10 9 8 7 6 5 4 3 2 1

ISBN 0 431 02210 0 (paperback)
09 08 07 06 05
10 9 8 7 6 5 4 3 2 1

British Library Cataloguing in Publication Data
Barraclough, Sue
What can I? – See
612.8'4
A full catalogue record for this book is available from the British Library.

Acknowledgements
The Publishers would like to thank the following for permission to reproduce photographs: Alamy / Copson City Pictures pp.**10-11**; Alamy / Imagestate p.**12**; Bryant-Mole Books p.**9**; Corbis / Collections p.**13**; Digital Stock p.**15** top; Getty Images / Imagebank pp.**20-21**; Getty Images / PhotoDisc pp.**14** inset, **15** bottom, **19** all images; Harcourt Education pp.**9** top (Chris Honeywell), **4-5**, **6**, **7**, **8**, **22-23** (Tudor Photography); Photolibrary p.**17** inset (OSF); PhotoVault pp.**14-15**; Powerstock pp.**16-17**; Powerstock / Brand X Pictures p.**18**.

Cover photograph reproduced with permission of Harcourt Education Ltd. / Tudor Photography.

Every effort has been made to contact copyright holders of any material reproduced in this book. Any omissions will be rectified in subsequent printings if notice is given to the Publishers.

Contents

Wake up!

It is time to open
your eyes.

Wakey, wakey!

Choosing colours

Can you see the different coloured T-Shirts?

Orange or green?

What is your **favourite** colour?

Where are we going?

Can you **guess** where we are going?

Beside the sea

What colour is
the sea?

11

Buckets and spades

Our sandcastle will be **huge!**

What can you see in the rockpool?

Splish!

Splash!

Can you see what people are wearing to protect them from the sun?

I spy...

Telescopes help us to see things that are **far away**.

Can you describe
what the children
are looking at?

15

Ice cream hunt

On a **hot** day, it's good to stop for an **ice cream!**

Can you find an ice cream?

Yummy!

Brilliant fish

There are two **bright, stripy** fish. Can you see the pink fish?

bubble

How many different colours
and patterns can you see?

Night sky

The moon and stars are **bright** in the sky. How many stars can you count?

Index

Notes for adults

This series encourages children to explore their environment to gain knowledge and understanding of the things they can see, smell, hear, taste, and feel. The following Early Learning Goals are relevant to the series:

• use the senses to explore and learn about the world around them
• respond to experiences and describe, express, and communicate ideas
• make connections between new information and what they already know
• ask questions about why things happen and how things work
• discover their local environment and talk about likes and dislikes.

The following additional information may be of interest
The eyes detect colours and patterns of light and send this information to the brain in the form of nerve signals. Sight is one of the most important senses because the eyes send a huge amount of different information to the brain.

Follow-up activities
As part of a painting session encourage children to look carefully at an object and discuss and describe all the information that their eyes provide – colours, light and shade, shape and size – before they start to paint.